a WALK in WASCANA

A park called Wascana welcomes you
with shining water and skies of blue.

Verdant trees and brilliant sun...
it's a place for everyone.

A field of rabbits beckons you
to bypass bushes, sidestep through.
One bunny's wink seems to say
"I'll hide, you seek. Will you play?"

I'll wander pathways—
where's my friend?
Could bunny be around this bend?
Is she hiding in the leaves
or bounding past
the grand green trees?

Above the grass where sparrows play,
elm trees' leaves uplift and sway.
Is bunny here among the reeds,
where ducks and geese have come to feed?

Perhaps I'll leave a carrot treat—
a rabbit's favourite thing to eat.
Come out, bunny! Will you peek
and end this lively hide and seek?

Still want to play? Okay, why not?
Is bunny in this shady spot
where squirrels are romping all around,
eating morsels on the ground?

What other creatures can I meet
as I follow bunny's feet?

Mommy rabbit's looking too,
and busy bee has lots to do.

This muskrat is a welcome sight,
gliding in the prairie light.

Smoothly paddling, floating dreams,
underneath the sunny beams.

Of sprightly bunny still no sign
in leafy meadows, sun ashine.

Surging green on trees alight,
while trilling songbirds pause their flight.

Here where all these beings thrive,
my heart and senses come alive.
I have noticed, search aside,
nature makes me calm inside.

Firmly proud, a totem stands—
an image from our early land.
A cedar story, eagle-high,
ruler of the endless sky.

"Pile of bones," Wascana means.
The past is present in these scenes.
From many peoples' strength we grow,
as surely as the wind will blow.

In this quiet reverie,
I can let my thoughts float free.
Rising, reaching, climbing high,
lifting to the living sky.

I spy some brown—did bunny come?
There you are, my whiskered chum!
I was here just being me
under a leaf-lush canopy.

Little mate, I'll say goodbye.
I'm glad we shared the boundless sky
and sun-washed prairie 'neath our feet.
Farewell, my friend—again we'll meet.

HER MAJESTY QUEEN ELIZABETH II

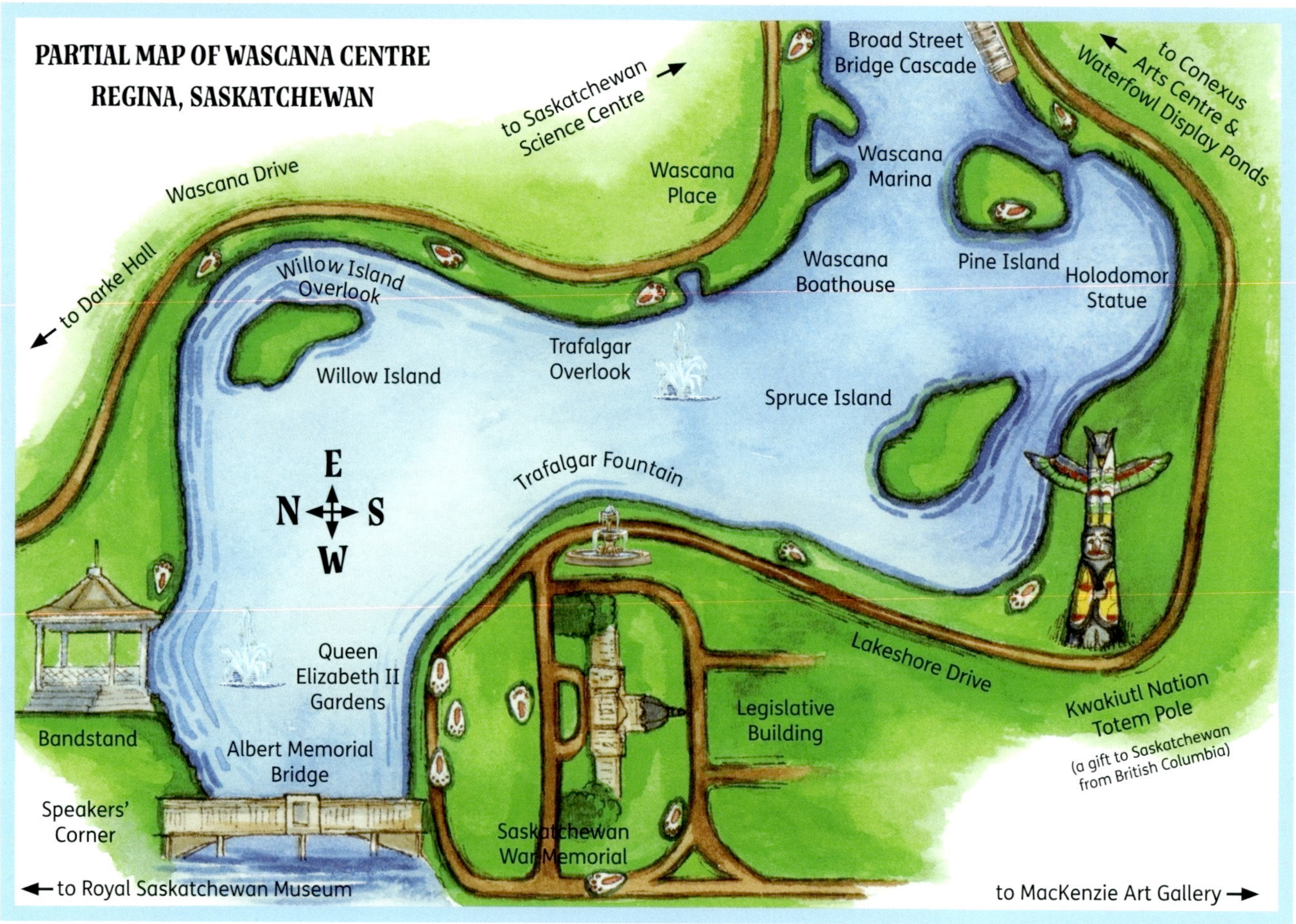

NOTE:

Regina was once prime bison-hunting territory for Indigenous peoples. The animal bones were gathered in piles along the creek, giving the area its Cree name: oskana kâ-asastêki, or Pile O'Bones. Wascana Centre, and most of southern Saskatchewan, is situated on Treaty 4 Territory, the ancestral lands of the Cree, Saulteaux and Assiniboine peoples, and homeland of the Métis. Saskatchewan's provincial motto is: *Multis e gentibus vires*—from many peoples, strength.

Published by Your Nickel's Worth Publishing.
June 2019

Cataloguing data available from Library and Archives Canada.

978-1-988783-40-6

Printed in Canada.
23 22 21 20 19 1 2 3 4 5

Book design by Heather Nickel.

YOUR NICKEL'S WORTH PUBLISHING
www.ynwp.ca